A Timeless Book

The Denali National Park branch of the Alaska Natural History Association is pleased to present this latest edition of *Mammals of Denali* by Adolph Murie.

This book was first printed in 1962 as *The Mammals of Mount McKinley*. When the park's name was changed to "Denali," the title of the book was also changed, but the text is still that of Adolph Murie, park biologist from 1939 and into the 1970s.

This book is very special to the Alaska Natural History Association as *The Mammals of Mount McKinley* was our first publication when we were known as the Mount McKinley Natural History Association. Currently, the Alaska Natural History Association has over thirty branches across the state and over twenty books in print.

At Denali National Park visitors can glimpse the drama of life in the wild. A ride on a park bus may reveal a grizzly mother nursing her cubs, a band of sheep grazing amongst the hills, or a wolf trotting back to its den.

Each year thousands of photographs are taken of these special Denali animals by amateurs and professionals. We would like to give a special thanks to the photographers who donated the use of their images for this edition of *Mammals of Denali*. Dorothy Keeler typifies all these photographers when she says, "My husband Leo and I get so much enjoyment from the park. This is our favorite place on Earth. Contributing to the book is our way of sharing and giving something back."

Over the years Adolph Murie's work has developed into a standard for succeeding biologists. His work in Denali on predator-prey relationships was ground-breaking and changed the way that biologists viewed predators, especially the wolf. The following pages reveal his love for wildlife existing in a natural state. We are fortunate to have his words to introduce us to the special place that is Denali National Park.

ALASKA
NATURAL HISTORY ASSOCIATION

Grizzly

Mammals of Denali

BY ADOLPH MURIE

FROM THE PUBLICATION
MAMMALS OF MOUNT MCKINLEY NATIONAL PARK, ALASKA

© 1962, 1994 by Alaska Natural History Association
Revised editions 1994, 1999

ISBN 0-930931-12-2

Published by the Alaska Natural History Association
in cooperation with the National Park Service.
Gina Soltis, Project Coordinator

For information write:
    Alaska Natural History Association
    P.O. Box 230
    Denali Park, Alaska 99755

Printed by the Donning Company/Publishers
Virginia Beach, Virginia
Steve Mull, General Manager
Barbara A. Bolton, Project Director
Tracey Emmons-Schneider, Project Research Coordinator
Lori Wiley, Art Director, Designer
Elizabeth B. Bobbitt, Production Editor

Contents

Lynx

Library of Congress Cataloging in Publication Data:
Murie, Adolph, 1899–1974
Mammals of Denali / by Adolph Murie. —Rev. Ed.
　　p.　　cm.
　Rev ed. of : Mammals of Mount McKinley National Park, Alaska.
　ISBN 0-930931-12-2
　1. Mammals—Alaska—Denali National Park and Preserve.
2. Denali National Park and Preserve (Alaska) I. Murie, Adolph,
1899–1974 Mammals of Mount McKinley National Park, Alaska.
II. United States. National Park Service. III. Title.
QL719.A55M8　1994
599.09798'3—dc20　　　　94-14061
　　　　　　　　　CIP
Printed in the United States of America

Acknowledgments

Photographers:

Steve Buskirk, 76, 77;

Leo Keeler, 36, 40, 48, 64;

Rick McIntyre, front cover, 22, 25, 50, 52, 54;

National Park Service, Denali, 71, 80;

Mary Ostermick, 29;

Rollie Ostermick, 2, 6, 12–13, 20, 34;

Charlie Ott, 4–5, 69;

Gerry Reynolds, 15, 31, 38;

David Rhode, 18, 28, 79;

Helen Rhode, back cover, 61, 66, 68, 74;

William Ruth, 58 (top);

Jim Shives, 57;

Tom Walker, 26, 59;

Kennan Ward, 10, 32, 42, 43, 44, 46, 58 (bottom), 72; and

Ed Zahniser, 8.

Bull moose in pond

Preface

This latest edition of Adolph Murie's original publication *Mammals of Mount McKinley National Park, Alaska* has been modified only slightly from the original. We have chosen to maintain Murie's personal style including its gracious language, anthropomorphic qualities, and extensive use of masculine pronouns.

The expansion and renaming of Mount McKinley National Park to Denali National Park and Preserve have necessitated modifying some of Murie's descriptions when located in reference to park boundaries. The name change, of course, has also resulted in the new title of this publication.

In the thirty-seven years since its original publication, many aspects of the natural history of the park have followed their natural course. As a result, some of Murie's references to population numbers are not accurate today. In particular, the reader should be aware that today's best estimates place the total number of caribou in the park at about 2,000 animals and the total number of Dall sheep in the park at about 2,200 animals. In addition, some taxonomic and common names have been changed where necessary to keep the book up to date with newer authoritative references. These names have been changed to agree with the U.S. government's Integrated Taxonomic Information System (ITIS). Common names of birds, where specific, are named in accordance with the 41st supplement to the A.O.U. Checklist of North American Birds.

It is our intent that these few changes will provide the reader with accurate information at no penalty to Murie's exceptional and authoritative work. The historic observations and compassionate descriptions of this pioneering ecologist have value of their own which we all can enjoy today.

About the Author

Adolph Murie has come to be regarded as much more than simply the foremost researcher of the ecology of Denali National Park. He now is part of the essential lore. He and his brother Olaus, together with their respective wives, Louise and Margaret (who happened to be sisters), made Alaska and Denali the focus of much of their enduring interest and energy. Adolph spent twenty-five summers here starting in 1929 and ending in 1970. During much of that time, he and his family lived in the tiny, one-room East Fork cabin. Adolph was a familiar sight throughout the park as he observed, described, analyzed, and recorded the wealth of information summarized in this book.

Trained as a professional scientist, he was also a sensitive and eloquent writer. Adolph Murie died in 1974. These writings carry on his deep concern for Denali National Park and the creatures he wrote about so caringly.

Olaus and Adolph Murie

WARNING

RESTRICTED
WILDLIFE AREA

FOR NEXT 5 MILES PHOTOGRAPHY
AND OBSERVATION OF WILDLIFE
PERMITTED FROM ROAD ONLY

Grizzly sow and cubs

Denali Wilderness

The national park idea represents a far-reaching cultural achievement, for here we raise our thoughts above the average, and enter a sphere in which the intangible values of the human heart and spirit take precedence. Mingled with the landscape of Denali National Park is the spirit of the primeval. The region is dedicated to the preservation of wilderness. Here we try to refrain from the coarser uses of nature legitimate elsewhere.

All the plants and animals enjoy a natural and normal life without human restrictions. Freedom prevails—the foxes are free to dig burrows where they will; to hunt ptarmigan, ground squirrels and mice as the spirit moves; and they share in the ownership of the blueberry and crowberry patches. The grizzlies wander over their ancestral home unmolested; dig roots and ground squirrels, graze grass, and harvest berries according to whatever menu appeals to them. The "bad" wolf seeks an honest living as of yore; he is a respected citizen, morally on a par with everyone else. His hunting of mice, ground squirrels, caribou and Dall sheep is his way of life and he has the freedom to follow it. No species of plant is favored above the rest, and they grow together, quietly competing, or living in adjusted composure. Our task is to perpetuate this freedom and purity of nature, this ebb and flow of life—first, by insuring ample park boundaries so that the region is large enough to maintain the natural relationships, and secondly, to hold man's intrusions to the minimum.

Most of us feel with Thoreau that "The wilderness is near as well as dear to every man." We come to Denali to watch; to catch a glimpse of the primeval. We come close to the tundra flowers, the lichens, and the animal life. Each of us will take some inspiration home; a touch of the tundra will enter our lives—and, deep inside, make of us all poets and kindred spirits.

Our national parks, here in the north, are set aside, not only for Alaskans, or for Americans, but for all humanity. To preserve the delicate charm and the wildness of the region our thoughts must be guided by a morality encompassing the spiritual welfare of the universe.

Caribou

The Denali region was set aside as a national park in 1917. The foresighted conservationists who advocated national park status for this country were activated chiefly by their desire to preserve the flora and fauna it its pristine condition. An effort was made to give the park ample boundaries, and desirable extensions were later made to preserve the entire mountain massif and assure a self-sustaining ecological unit.

A drive from the Nenana River, the eastern boundary, to Wonder Lake, some 90 miles to the west and directly north of Mount McKinley (called Denali by interior Indians), is always a fresh adventure. No two days are the same. One day we may see more grizzlies than usual; on another trip we may be especially fortunate and catch sight of a wolf or a wolverine. It is desirable to travel slowly and to stop occasionally to examine the landscape for animal life—the mountains for Dall sheep, the river bars and passes for grizzlies and caribou, and the water for birds, beaver, or moose.

Some of the birds to be seen along the way are the ptarmigan— willow ptarmigan in the low country, rock ptarmigan on the high passes (the white-tailed are confined to higher elevations and probably will not be seen)—the long-tailed jaegers, the whimbrels, American golden-plovers, mew gulls, golden eagles, and several kinds of ducks. Ornithologists will be especially interested in seeing such Asiatic birds as the wheatear and the arctic warbler.

Much of the park is treeless tundra, but strips of woods follow the rivers far into the park, and patches grow here and there on the adjacent mountain slopes. Timberline varies according to soil and exposure; in places it reaches elevations of over 3,500 feet.

White spruce is the common conifer. Black spruce is confined to poorly drained and boggy areas. Along the north boundary I have seen a few patches of tamarack. Balsam poplar and aspen are widely distributed, and a few tree birches grow at lower elevations. Along the McKinley River an extensive strip of balsam poplar may be seen from the highway.

The tundra supports a growth of willow and dwarf birch. Over twenty-five kinds of willow occur in the park. They range in size from small forms only two or three inches in height, to brushy growths twenty

Arctic ground squirrel

feet tall. In places the small willows may grow dense enough to form a sod. These shrubs are highly important for wildlife. Alder brush is widely distributed and plentiful on canyon slopes; near Wonder Lake there are many clumps of alder in the rolling tundra.

The low ground cover over the park consists of mosses, lichens, sedges, grasses, horsetails, and herbaceous plants—many species of each. Early flowers may begin blooming in late April and early May, and at the higher elevations some blooms may be seen in late summer.

The annual berry crop is bounteous and is an important source of food for a host of birds and mammals. Even the mountain sheep have been found enjoying the blueberries. Blueberry, crowberry, cranberry, buffaloberry, and alpine bearberry are all widely distributed. The berries begin to ripen in late July.

With the melting of the snow in the spring, the white landscape of winter is transformed into a brown countryside—brown grasses, sedges, and leafless shrubbery. Snow fields still persist on the mountain slopes, and the spruces are dark green, but brown hues seem to dominate one's impression of the tundra at this time. In June—the time varies a little with the year—the landscape is magically transformed from a dull brown to the brightest green. Early in August spots of red and yellow colors begin to show. By late August and early September the country is again transformed and we have a world of crimson and other shades of red, trimmed with yellow and gold of willow, aspen, and balsam poplar. The alders add contrast for they remain summer-green throughout the autumn color season.

Over much of the country the ground remains frozen below a depth of a few feet. In some shaded areas where the ground is deeply carpeted with moss, the soil remains frozen within less than two feet of the surface. The continuous thawing of the soil in summer keeps the surface moist until autumn. The thawed surface soil tends in places to creep imperceptibly down slopes as it becomes water-soaked, even though plant life has a strong stabilizing influence. Occasionally the soil becomes saturated with moisture to considerable depths and we have rather large landslides with slides such as the one that shows prominently on the south slope of Sable Mountain; and one to the south of the road at about 3-Mile that caused spruces to lean in various directions. Thawed, water-logged surface soil rests uneasily on the frozen sub-stratum.

A number of parallel, northward-flowing streams head in glaciers lying along the north slope of the Alaska Range. The streams are not large—most of them can be waded without getting too wet—so it is surprising to find them bordered by wide gravel bars. This is due to lack of stream stabilization. In summer the streams carry a load of silt which may be dropped along the way. Channels are continually being gouged out here and filled in somewhere else so that the stream keeps breaking over its sides and forming additional channels. High water, due to a warm day and much glacier melting, or to heavy rains, may cause the streams to flow into entirely new channels. When the main stream reaches the side of the gravel bar it will erode the bank and thus broaden the river bar. This type of erosion is noticeable just below the Teklanika Bridge. Gravel bars that have not been invaded for a long period may become covered with vegetation, and it is on some of these old bars that we often see grizzlies digging roots in the spring of the year. But even these bars are temporary. One such bar on the Toklat River was invaded by part of the river a few years ago and much of the sod is being washed away today. Physiographic processes are all very active in the region. On many slopes we see the turf breaking away, and here and there a small land slip.

Those who come to the park the early part of the summer may see extensive fields of ice on the river bars. These are the result of what is called overflow. During cold weather the ice on the streams freezes so thick that there is not room for all of the water to pass under the ice, and since it must run somewhere, it develops pressure and breaks out on the surface where it spreads widely underneath the snow. Here it freezes. This process continues throughout the winter and often forms ice patches many feet thick. When one is dog-mushing on rivers the overflow water under the snow is a hazard before it freezes, and the driver of a dogteam must watch to avoid such spots. Conditions are worst during the coldest weather, at a time when a wetting is most serious.

Out in the park there are no trails. The country is so open that trails are not needed. The river bars furnish excellent hiking, and even walking across the upland tundra is easy. A number of campgrounds are located along the road between the Nenana River and Wonder Lake.

This booklet is made available as a quick reference pertaining to the mammals in the park. The comments on each species are brief but perhaps sufficient to suggest their status. Distances are deceiving, so field glasses should be used in searching the landscape for the larger animals such as sheep, caribou, and bears.

Grizzly

Grizzly Bear

URSUS ARCTOS

The grizzly's domain in the park extends from the glaciers at the heads of the rivers, northward to the north boundary. The grizzly may be discovered on an old river bar, on one of the low passes between the rivers, or traveling high on a mountain slope. One of the favorite haunts along the road is Sable Pass, where each summer one to four females with cubs, along with a few lone or mated bears, take residence.

Any bear seen out in the park is almost certain to be a grizzly because the black bear is confined to the wooded low country along the east and north boundaries. The hump on the shoulder and the dishfaced profile (rather than almost straight, as in the black bear) are good field characters. The general coloration varies from cream color (rare) to straw color, brown, chocolate, and black. The legs are always blackish. The fur fades considerably during the spring and summer. Hence, the new coat, fully developed by autumn, is always darker, and gives the bear a new, fresh look. One old male grizzly, not very fat, weighed 650 pounds. The females are considerably smaller. Because of the long claws on the forepaws, the track of the grizzly can be readily distinguished from that of the black bear, whose forepaw claws are shorter and more curved.

In the spring, when grizzlies first come forth from their dens, they seem to do much wandering over the higher slopes. At this season I have noted their tracks leading to the remains of sheep, caribou, and moose that had succumbed during the winter. Usually the wolves, foxes, and wolverines have long since feasted on the fleshy parts, but the bears are happy to crush the bones that remain on the premises and thus obtain a taste of the succulent marrow.

The spring and early-summer food is chiefly the root of the peavine (*Hedysarum alpinum americanum*) that flourishes on old vegetated river bars and on many mountain slopes. Using both paws, with their long

claws, and straining backward with his body weight, chunks of sod are turned over to expose the thick peavine roots. With delicate strokes, his paws further expose the roots, which taste much like the garden variety of pea. So expensive is the root digging at times that an area may look like a plowed field when the bear has finished. At this season, because of these food habits, bears can often be seen on the open river bars and on the ridge slopes. Cranberries and crowberries that have wintered under the snow are often eaten in spring.

In June, green vegetation becomes available and a drastic change of diet results. The root digging is terminated for something better. A grass (*Arctagrostis latifolia*), with a stiff and juicy stalk, and growing in swales and wettish areas, is a favorite. The bears also graze extensively on horsetail (*Equisetem arvense*), mountain-sorrel (*Oxyria digyna*), and the tall showy white saxifrage (*Boykinia richardsonii*). A pea (*Oxytropis viscida*), growing abundantly far up the streams on old river bars, is extensively grazed.

The grizzly is quite fastidious in his feeding on dock (*Rumex arcticus*). He severs the thick juicy stem with a bite and as he chews, the large reddish seed head drops from his lips, neatly discarded.

The grizzlies continue grazing and chomping green grasses and herbs until berry time when another major change of food habits takes place. Some grazing still persists, but now the bears turn wholeheartedly to blueberries, crowberries, and the bitter scarlet buffaloberries, the three species of berries most abundant and available. The lush berry of *Arctostaphylous rubra*, that ground-hugging woody plant that colors patches of the landscape a brilliant scarlet in autumn, are sometimes eaten, but not with any efficiency. The berry diet continues through the autumn, but at this season a few roots may again be sought.

The bear belongs to the order *Carnivora* and yet little mention has been made of meat in the diet. He is perhaps, so to speak, a victim of evolution and has had to adjust. As his mature size became ever larger through eons of time, he became too slow to catch large herbivores such as the caribou, and his large body required more sustenance than could be secured by digging for mice and ground squirrels under usual circumstances. Therefore he had to turn more and more to vegetation which could be secured in quantity. This is not as drastic a change as we might offhand suppose. It is one chiefly of degree, because we find carnivores such as the fox and the marten turning to a berry diet for a period, from choice.

But it appears that the grizzly would like more meat than is generally available. This I infer from the quantity he eats when he finds a carcass and from the avidity with which bears of all kinds seek spawning fish when available. The only animal that the grizzly consistently hunts in the park is the ground squirrel, but a squirrel contributes only

Grizzly sow
nursing cubs

a mouthful and its capture usually requires excessive time and energy. Sometimes a squirrel is surprised and captured before it can disappear in a burrow. But generally a squirrel is secured only after extensive excavating which may involve as much as half an hour, and not infrequently the bear, after much digging, fails to unearth his intended victim. In years when meadow mice and lemmings are especially abundant, bears may make their capture a project which contributes at least a tasty diversion. Caribou and moose calves may occasionally be captured when very young, but the season for this food is short. Occasionally tidings come to a bear's keen nose that carrion lies upwind, and the lucky bear keeps gorging until only a few bones and patches of hide remain.

After feeding on a carcass the bear often covers it with sod and vegetation. One fall at Stony Creek I watched a bear at a cache which showed up as a dark mound surrounded by a dark circular area from which the sod had been torn loose. For an hour the bear kept methodically raking the surrounding area beyond.

He was scraping the loose vegetation toward the cache, working leisurely with one paw at a time. The loosened material was pushed toward the cache as the work progressed. When I examined the area later, I noted a circular patch, extending out twenty feet from all sides of the carcass, that had been combed clean of loose vegetation. The bear finally lay on the cache to wait for digestion to create more space for this rich fare.

North of Wonder Lake a grizzly had similarly covered a caribou that a hunter had left lying in the field. The bear was not at the cache, but since most of the carcass was still intact, he probably was not far away. I found some carcasses that were not covered with sod. A mother and two yearlings at Polychrome Pass left a caribou carcass without covering it and retired to some steep cliffs overlooking the area. The following day they rested near the carcass, but still no effort was made to cover it.

Mating takes place in May, June, and early July, and a pair remains together for two or three weeks. I suspect that a male might look for a second marriage following the termination of the first. One large, crippled male was successfully consorting with two females at the same time, neither female objecting to the presence of the other—in fact, both probably preferred it that way.

The cubs are born in the hibernating den in midwinter, are eight or nine inches long, and weigh less than two pounds at birth. The number of cubs in a litter ordinarily varies from one to three, two being the most frequent.

The cubs not only nurse throughout the first summer, but to about the same extent during their second summer abroad, when they are robust yearlings. I had been surprised to find yearlings regularly nursing, but it was a greater surprise to observe mother grizzlies nursing cubs over two years old, in their third summer abroad. The protracted nursing period indicates a breeding interval of females with cubs, of three or more years, since females followed by nursing yearlings have not been seen consorting with a male.

The dens used for hibernation are excavated by the grizzly if natural caves are not available. A den is usually dug on a rather steep slope. The entrance to one I examined was about two feet wide and a little less than two and one-half feet high. A tunnel six feet long led to the chamber which was roughly four feet in diameter. Cinquefoil brush and grass had been used for the bed. This den was still usable six years after it was dug. But another den dug in October caved in the following summer. It lacked the firm protective sod roof of the more durable den.

Bears, like humans, enjoy a good back-scratching. Trees along a trail or on some strategic point are much used, as shown by the rubbing signs and the adhering hairs. If trees are not available, willow brush, a boulder, or a sod bank may be used. The corner of a log cabin is considered an excellent surface. A pole lying on the ground is a fair substitute, and where no structure is available and a bear feels itchy he may lie on the ground with all four feet in the air, wriggling ludicrously with excessive energy to do the job.

Generally the grizzlies wander freely over the tundra. But they are not averse to taking advantage of a convenient trail when they have a definite destination. Trails that are much used by bears, such as we sometimes find along the bank of a river or through a woods, show a series of worn depressions. These depressions are due to the grizzlies' tendency to step in the same tracks. They no doubt have been formed by the passage of many bears over a long period.

The grizzly has survived in only a few states, more by accident than by our planning for his future. In Alaska we have a great opportunity for giving the grizzly and the rest of the fauna ample room for carrying on their living in a natural, free manner. The grizzly needs extensive wilderness country for his way of life, and wild country is also vital for the highest development of human culture. If we provide for the future of the grizzly, we at the same time provide wilderness for our own needs.

Black Bear

URSUS AMERICANUS

The black bear is widely distributed in Alaska. In the park it is confined to the forested areas along the north and east boundaries. I have occasionally seen one near the Nenana River and in the Wonder Lake area I have seen them three or four miles north of the lake feeding on blueberries.

Black bears may be black or brown, but those I have seen at Denali have all been of the black color phase. The black bear lacks the pronounced shoulder hump of the grizzly. The tan muzzle is also distinctive. Equipped with strong, curved claws, the black bear climbs trees with surprising agility, a talent the grizzly seems to lack.

Black bear

The food habits of the black bear are similar to those of the grizzly, but in general they spend more time turning over rocks and tearing apart logs in search of insect life. They feed on herbs and grass, are fond of berries, hunt mice and dig out ground squirrels, and are ever on the alert for carrion. In the Rocky Mountains and on the West Coast, they occasionally strip the bark from trunks of spruces, pines, and firs in order to feed on the inner cambium layer. Along the coast of Alaska they sometimes congregate to feed on spawning salmon.

Where we have bears we have potential bear problems. Roadside feeding of bears creates beggar bears—always dangerous. Allowing bears to obtain food in cabins or camps demoralizes them, encourages them in a life of plunder and general anti-human depredations—the usual outcome is damage to humans and the death of the bears. A point of view generally disregarded by all is the effect of garbage on the bears. No garbage should be made available to bears anywhere for the simple reason that such artificial food interferes with the natural feeding habits of bears and their natural distribution, tending to congregate large numbers of them in a limited area. Administrators and public alike must ever be heedful of the problem. Clean campsites and proper garbage disposal are desirable in this regard.

Caribou cow and calf

Caribou

RANGIFER TARANDUS

The caribou is a circumpolar deer adapted to life in the Arctic. Both sexes carry antlers, and even the calves grow a spike six or eight inches long. The cow's antlers are small and branching; those of the old bull are towering and picturesque, with a well-developed brow tine extending over the nose from one or both antlers. As you see the caribou in his easy swinging trot, you will perhaps notice his big feet. The hoofs, rounded and spreading, and the dew claws well developed, serve him as snowshoes in winter, and as a broad support in the soft tundra.

Each spring the caribou appear in faded, dun coats, their color pattern gone, the long hair worn and frayed. Winter hardships are behind and the sprouting, nutritious, vitamin-packed green forage is available—nature's restorative. On the hummocks the caribou are already finding the new growth of sedge hidden by the old, leached, brown blades. As the winter coat is shed, and the new black pelage shows in patches, the animals have a moth-eaten look.

In May and early June, the caribou that have wintered along the north boundary of the park and northward to Lake Minchumina, move into the park, continue eastward to the Teklanika and Sanctuary rivers, and cross to the south side of the Alaska Range over the glaciers at the heads of these rivers. At this time the bands are small, numbering from a few individuals to one or two hundred. After feeding on the south side of the range for two or three weeks, the caribou return en masse, usually in late June or early July, but in 1960 about the middle of June. Herds numbering one or two thousand are not unusual, and I have seen an assemblage of four or five thousand. The herds cross Sable Pass and travel parallel with the road to Muldrow Glacier. From there they may strike northward or continue on westward. In August and September at least a few caribou may be found, especially in the Wonder Lake area.

Caribou are inordinately fond of lichens which they eagerly feed

Bull caribou

upon at all seasons. In summer they take advantage of the variety of foods available and feed extensively on grasses, many herbaceous species, willows, and lichens. Lichens are much sought in fall and winter, and in these seasons grasses and sedges continue to be major foods.

Caribou are plagued by warble flies and nostril flies throughout the summer. These beelike insects cause the caribou great annoyance. The warble fly lays eggs on the hair of the legs and underparts of the body. The eggs soon hatch, the larvae penetrate the hide, and move to the back region where they emerge as swollen larvae in the spring. The nostril flies deposit living larvae in the nostrils. The larvae become lodged back in the throat in a mass and the following spring are coughed out; they pupate on the ground, and soon emerge as terrorizing flies. A caribou may dash away in panic to escape a fly, then stop in a wet sedgy depression and hold its nose close to the ground. Thus it may stand for long periods if not attacked. On sunny days when the flies are very active, the movement of the herds is drastically influenced. The large herds may seek a high, breezy ridge, or a snowfield, to minimize the attack. Commonly, one or two thousand on such days assemble in a compact group on a broad gravel bar where they may stand all day. Should clouds cover the sun, the herd disperses to feed, but again converges if the sun reappears.

By midsummer the old hair has been shed and the caribou are in a short blackish coat that continues to grow. Not until September is this new pelage fully developed. By then it has become a rich chocolate brown, trimmed with white. The pattern is most striking in the old bulls. A silvery cape covers the neck and part of the shoulders and forms a mane on the throat. A white line extends back along the sides of the body, and the belly is white. The blunt nose is tipped with white and an oval white patch surrounds the tail. A white patch shows the location of the upper gland on the hind legs. White anklets border each shiny black hoof. The pattern is similar, but much more subdued, in the cows and younger bulls.

The magnificent antlers of the old bulls have hardened by late August. The velvet covering them during their growth is now rubbed off with a vigor suggesting the oncoming rut. At first the white antlers

Bull caribou battling

are often stained pinkish by the blood in the velvet. Continued rubbing on the brush removes the pinkish color and the antlers develop to a rich brown.

The bulls begin to spar soon after rubbing off the velvet. Even before serious fighting occurs, a bull may show his superiority to some of his companions. At this time two strange bulls do not hesitate to approach each other and, with no preliminaries, join antlers and try to drive each other back. These early fights are brief and on a more or less friendly basis. A sharp prong may cause a bull to pull away and be unwilling to resume sparring. But later, when a bull has acquired cows, up to a dozen or two, he herds them constantly, and fights all challengers.

The single reddish calf is generally born in May. His strength and speed develop rapidly so that he is soon able to follow the herds in their hurried travels. By autumn he has acquired a coat similar to that of the adults.

A close relationship exists between the caribou and the wolf, one that has prevailed for thousands of years. Although the wolf largely subsists on caribou over much of the north, natural adjustments have prevailed so that caribou have prospered in the presence of wolf populations. Wolves prey extensively on caribou calves during the spring. When a wolf takes after a herd of caribou containing calves, both old and young hold their own for a time. But soon a calf may begin to fall behind the racing herd, its endurance not quite up to that of the others. It is overtaken and eliminated. Natural selection has operated, a culling operation that over eons of time would seem to have evolutionary significance.

Grizzly bears capture a few very young calves. Encouraged by their early-season success they continue chasing calves long after the calves have gained strength and speed enough to readily escape. After a few failures, I suspect that a grizzly learns that the calf-catching season has passed and is no longer tempted to gallop ponderously and fruitlessly with excess power but not sufficient fleetness to capture fleeing calves.

(Note: As of 1998, there were two thousand caribou in the Denali Caribou herd.)

Moose

ALCES ALCES

The northern conifer forest, stretching across the continent, is the home of the moose. In Alaska he has reached his greatest size. A mature bull weighs twelve to fifteen hundred pounds, and his huge, palmate antlers have reached a record spread of about eighty inches.

At a distance the moose appears to be black except for his long, light-colored stockings. The large head is supported on a short neck, a shoulder hump is prominent, the nose is loose and bulbous. A special feature is the bell that hangs from the throat. The legs are inordinately long and the hoofs sharp.

Moose may be discovered anywhere along the park road. They are frequently to be seen between Savage and Sanctuary rivers, and along Igloo Creek. In the Igloo Creek area three or four old bulls may gener-

Bull moose battling

ally be found spending the summer together, their daily movements usually covering about a half-mile or less. We speak of the moose as a forest animal, but it is often found the year round in willow brush beyond timber. It is not uncommon to see moose in the willows on the treeless passes such as Sable and Polychrome.

The principal food of the moose is browse. In summer the leaves are stripped from the branches; at other seasons the twigs are eaten. Willows and dwarf birch are the chief browse species in the park. Aspens and balsam poplar are relished but are not plentiful enough to be very important. Alder is generally eaten only sparingly in winter. Farther south over the moose's range, firs and hemlock are highly palatable in winter. The long legs enable the moose to reach high in his browsing. It is not unusual to find winter browsing sign twelve feet or more from the ground where the moose have stood on snow to feed. Tall willow brush and aspen saplings are often broken over in order to get at the twigs out of reach. The muzzle may be used for this, or the

Cow moose and calf

limb may be grasped in the mouth and pulled down. Many broken willows are evident on the bars along Igloo Creek.

The long legs and short neck make grazing difficult. In Wyoming, I once saw a cow and calf feeding on mushrooms, a delicacy. Reaching the ground was not easy—the calf dropped to his knees, and the cow was for part of the time down on one knee.

In summer, moose may be seen in lakes and ponds feeding on submerged vegetation. Where the water is deep the moose may disappear below the surface in his feeding.

Rutting activities begin in the first of September and continue into October. The antlers of the bulls have reached full size and hardened by the end of August, at which time the bulls begin to rub off the velvet, the skin that has covered the growing antlers. Saplings and brush are thrashed with great vigor, and this activity continues long after the antlers have been cleaned. Apparently it serves as one of the outlets for the strong rutting emotions. The bulls soon begin to spar and to determine who is boss over whom. And they begin to seek the cows. A successful bull usually has several cows. He will follow a cow closely as she moves about in her feeding. During the rut he utters at intervals a deep grunt. The cow, apparently when in an emotional state, utters a drawn-out wailing call.

The one or two calves are generally born in late May or early June. They are reddish without spots. The mother must sometimes protect her calf from prowling grizzlies and this she generally seems fully capable of doing, judging from incidents in which the bear is chased away by an infuriated mother. A large male grizzly, however, is apparently not easily discouraged. By autumn the calves have made a surprising growth and have a new coat that resembles that of the adults. They remain with the mother until near the time for a new calf, when she no longer tolerates their presence.

The moose is a wilderness animal, requiring for his haunts big country. The picturesque bull, silhouetted on a hill or on a lake shore, adds repose and serenity to the wilderness.

Dall Sheep

OVIS DALLI

The Dall or white sheep is one of the outstanding wildlife features of the park. The north side of the greater part of the Alaska Range is excellent sheep habitat. Within the park the most extensive sheep country extends from the Nenana River to the Muldrow Glacier, a distance of about seventy miles by road.

Most of the sheep spend the winter north of the road. This is favorable winter range because the snowfall is relatively light and strong winds keep the exposed ridges free of snow.

Many sheep remain on the winter range all year, but more of them migrate toward the heads of the rivers in May and June. In making the migration, the sheep must in places cross two or three miles of low country. They are fully aware of their vulnerability to grizzlies and wolves in these crossings. Before venturing away from the safe take-off ridge, they may scrutinize the low country for a day or two, until they feel that no danger lurks along the way. A band of sixty or seventy sheep may move across slowly in a rather compact group; at other times urgency replaces caution and they frequently break into a hurried gallop. Having reached the safety of rough country again, the sheep may gambol about as though the weight of tension has suddenly been lifted. The return migration is made in August and September.

The large amber-colored horns of the rams, with transverse ridges and sweeping outward curl, have a rugged, graceful beauty. They may spread widely at the tips or curl rather close to the head. The ewes are less imposing. Their horns are slender spikes that extend upward in a slight curve, resembling those of the mountain goat, but they lack the shiny jet black color and are not as sharp. The horns are never shed and continue to grow throughout the sheep's life span of eleven to fourteen years. The growth is slight during the later years. Growth takes place during the summer when food is highly nutritious. In winter, only a

Dall sheep ram

groove or ridge encircling the horn is formed. By counting these annual rings the age of a sheep can be determined.

For detecting danger the sheep depend on their sharp eyes. They appear to disregard scent, which for many animals is the final decisive word on any situation. But this seems quite logical, because the sheep generally have a strategic view, and in the varying air currents no dependence can be placed on getting scent messages. Noises are considered rather unimportant unless the sheep have already caught a glimpse of movement nearby.

Dall sheep ewe and lamb

To approach sheep for photography it is usually best to move slowly toward them from below with no attempt to hide. They at once become suspicious if they glimpse someone stalking. However, I have at times stalked sheep where the opportunity for undetected close observation was obvious. On one occasion, from a ragged rocky ridge top, I spent most of an afternoon watching a band of rams some fifty yards away without being discovered. Some bands are wilder than others and the same band does not always behave uniformly. A band that has rested and is ready to move may take your approach as an excuse for a romp.

The food of sheep consists of grasses, herbaceous species and browse, chiefly willow. Scattered over the range are a number of salt licks which the sheep seek for minerals.

The most active mating period extends from about the middle of November to the middle of December. The rams who have been fraternizing on friendly terms for many months, now and then showing mating behavior such as gentle joustings, begin to take greater notice of the ewes. The old rams continue to associate, but now serious battling takes place. The fighting follows rather uniform, conventional rules. The two matched battlers move apart several yards, then, as though by a signal, they turn and face each other and at the same time raise up on their hind legs, then charge full speed at each other, their horns crashing together with a loud thud. If the joust is even, they may repeat the performance until the superiority of one of the combatants is evident. But there is some tolerance among the rams, for two or more may breed with ewes in a band indiscriminately.

The number of sheep on a range under natural conditions may vary considerably. In the park, a very high population, possibly as high as five thousand or more, suffered severe losses during 1929 and again in 1932, due to extremely deep snow conditions, and an icy crust in the latter year. In 1945 the population was down to about five hundred. Since 1945 there has been a steady increase. The number in 1959 was up to about two thousand.

Sheep are subject to wolf predation, especially when the numbers are so high that part of the population must graze on hills too gentle for safety. Sheep legs are strong and sturdy but for their effective functioning steep country is needed. The steep terrain is, so to speak, part of their legs. In my studies in the park, the losses showed that it was the very old, the ailing, and the lambs in their first winter that were most vulnerable to predation. The lynx (when hare numbers have crashed and these animals have become scarce), wolverine, and grizzly may capture an occasional sheep but their effect is unimportant. The golden eagle may capture an occasional young lamb, but all my observations and food-habit studies indicate that any eagle predation that takes place is insignificant. If the park is large enough to support the sheep and their predators (natural conditions), we have a situation ideal for the future of the sheep.

Mountain sheep have a high esthetic appeal. In part this may be due to their setting, for we associate them with their beautiful haunts, the precipitous cliffs and ledges intermingled with green slopes and spangled with flowers. This is idyllic country in which to hike and climb. Here we encounter the golden eagle who shares the ridge tops with the sheep; the wheatear, who comes all the way from Asia to nest; the gray-crowned rosy finches; the flashing black and white snow bunting nesting in rock crevices; and the surfbird that has left the ocean beaches to nest in these remote mountains. And up high, the saxifrages, delicate yellow poppies, forget-me-nots, and spring beauties add color to it all.

(Note: As of 1998, there were twenty-two hundred Dall sheep in Denali National Park.)

Mountain Goat

OREAMNOS AMERICANUS

On May 27, 1955, a goat was discovered on Igloo Mountain on the slope directly above the cabin I was occupying. It remained on the mountain for three weeks before wandering away. It has not been seen since. This is the only verified record for the park. But two road men reported seeing a goat cross the road at Mile 3, on August 8, 1950. I believe this to be a good record because both men are reliable observers. In the fall of 1950 a goat was shot at Cantwell, not far from the park boundary.

The nearest known goat range is about sixty miles from the park in the Talkeetna Mountains. The goats that reached the park may have been sporadic wanderers for it is not unusual for goats to occasionally wander twenty-five or thirty miles from their known ranges. On the other hand, it is possible that the goats are expanding their range toward the park. In 1959, I was told that a band of a dozen goats had been reported at the head of Jack River where they had not been reported before. Jack River lies between the goat range and the park.

Identification is not difficult. The goat's horns are short, slightly curved spikes, similar to the horns of the female sheep, but shiny black and smooth rather than grayish and rugose. The goat's chin whiskers are identifying, as is the shoulder hump, and the knee-length pantaloons of long hair. Also the goat's face is noticeably longer than that of sheep. The goat sexes are similar.

It is not unlikely that goats will continue to be occasionally seen in the park. Any lone "sheep" might turn out to be a goat.

Mountain goats

Wolf

CANIS LUPUS

Wolves vary considerably in size and color. The average male weighs about one hundred pounds and the female somewhat less, about eighty-five pounds. Their color may be almost white, black, gray, or brown. Most wolves in interior Alaska are either black or brownish like a coyote. The facial markings show some variation and there may occasionally be noticeable patterns over the rest of the body. A few wolves have a blackish saddle; one that I knew had a black robber-mask across the eyes. Individual disposition and behavior also vary. A handsome male had an extra touch of spirit in his gallop; a male parent had a dour expression and seemed, to my imagination, weighted with care.

For a den, the wolf considers an enlarged fox burrow both convenient and suitable. Dens have been found in a variety of situations. One was located on a wooded rock bluff, another was beyond timber near the top of a bluff bordering a river, and one was on a wooded island between old river channels. The four to six young, probably the average size litter, are born the early part of May. The mother remains at home with the pups and the male provides the victuals.

At one den that I observed closely there were two extra males and an extra female with the pair. These wolves all fraternized in the most friendly manner. Before departing for the night hunt, the five would sometimes assemble in a close group, wag tails and frisk about, and sitting on haunches sing in chorus. Later in the season this group of five adults was joined by two additional males.

The following year the same pair returned to the den. They were accompanied by one of the extra males that had been at the den the previous year. The extra female and one of the bachelors set up their own housekeeping farther down the river. But when their pups were large enough to travel, they all came up the river and joined the original pair. Young and old combined added up to fifteen wolves. This wolf pack was composed of two pairs, an extra adult, and ten pups. Some of the extra wolves of the previous year were not seen—they may have been trapped or poisoned beyond the park boundaries during the winter months.

The wolf's food varies with the seasons and the prey species available. When voles and lemmings are plentiful, the wolves may spend hours in the grass and sedge areas pouncing on them. During the summer months the ground squirrel has at times been one of the more important food items. Occasionally an unfortunate marmot is surprised and in years when hares are plentiful, the snowshoe hare becomes a food source. I have found remains of several porcupines eaten by wolves, the spine-covered hide nearly inverted.

But the wolf also, and primarily, feeds on the ungulates—the mountain sheep, caribou, and moose. Under natural conditions the relationship between the wolf and these prey species is old and tried. There is the aphorism, "nothing in nature offends nature." In the hunting of these animals the wolf appears to be an evolutionary force in that there is a tendency for the weaker individuals to succumb.

In the spring the wolf hunts the caribou calves, which early develop surprising speed, so that when a wolf chases a group of caribou, the calves race along with the adults. But after a time a weak calf, one not up to the others in endurance, may begin to drop behind, and it is this weak individual that is overtaken, an example of the elimination of the weak, the survival of the fittest. In the winter hunting, the old and weak animals are the most susceptible. It is a struggle, a testing for all, but through the ages, the sheep, moose, and caribou have survived and come down to us adapted to their particular way of life, with the wolf as one of the environmental factors.

Wolf

Wolf in fireweed

At Denali we have an opportunity to preserve a northern flora and fauna. But the future of the wolf is precarious because the home range of the park wolves extends beyond park boundaries. *(Note: Outside the park, as a furbearer and large game animal, the wolf can be trapped or hunted for sport and to sustain subsistence lifestyles. At times, wolf numbers in Alaska have also been reduced by predator control programs.)* The silencing of the longdrawn call of the wolf would be a tragic loss to the human spirit.

Coyote

Coyote

CANIS LATRANS

So far as known, the coyote has always been rare out in the park. Along the Nenana River, however, I frequently have heard his song. Here he seems to find conditions more favorable for his way of life. Perhaps it is the presence of the snowshoe hare in this low brushy country that attracts him.

The coyote weighs about twenty-five pounds on the average. His color is brownish with black-tipped hairs intermingled. Color variation in coyotes is so slight it is not noticeable in the field; he does not have the black, whitish, and various color patterns that are present in the wolf. The muzzle is long and pointed, ears well developed, eyes sharp.

As a field biologist I have had an opportunity to observe coyotes in many regions. In Yellowstone I made a two-year study of its relationships with other animals because it had been feared by some that he would destroy the antelope, bighorn, and deer, if not controlled. The study showed that the coyote there lived chiefly on meadow mice and pocket gophers in summer, and carrion in winter, and that he had no harmful effect on the large ungulates.

On the San Carlos Indian Reservation in Arizona the coyote was blamed for cattle losses. Here a study showed that the basic cause of losses was over-use of the range and that where grazing was good all losses were insignificant. Cattlemen are finding this true and are beginning to appreciate the usefulness of the coyote as a curbing influence on rodent depredations. In addition to a meat diet, which includes great quantities of grasshoppers in season, the coyote feeds extensively on fruit. On Isle Royale, in Lake Superior, I found it feeding on sarsaparilla berries; in Jackson Hole, Wyoming, on silverberry and quantities of haw; in Arizona, on manzanita and juniper berries, the latter being the winter staff of life.

The coyote is best known for his song, which in all its variations, symbolizes the spirit of wildness and remote country. J. Frank Dobie in his *The Voice of the Coyote* expresses the sentiment of many when he writes: "I confess to a sympathy for the coyote that has grown until it lives in the deepest part of my nature."

Red fox vixen with kit

Red Fox

VULPES VULPES

The fabled red fox is abundant, widely distributed over the park, and frequently seen. Silver, cross, and red color phases, along with some intermediate variants, are well represented, and two or three of these types frequently show up in a single litter. The prominent white tip on the tail distinguishes the fox from the coyote and wolf.

Hundreds of dens are scattered over the countryside, many more than are used in any one season. They are located indiscriminately in spruce woods and out on the open tundra miles from the nearest tree. Each pair has a selection of old dens to choose from, but often they occupy favorite sites year after year. During a season, a family sometimes moves from their first choice to a den nearby. The connecting burrows of a den usually have five or six entrances and one I examined had nineteen.

The young are born the early part of May. By June the blackish, blue-eyed, chubby pups may be seen walking about clumsily. At this age they are nursed in the open. One mother that I often watched almost always nursed her five pups from a standing position. Only twice did I see her lying on her side to nurse. As the pups grow they become slimmer and the eyes turn brown and the coat color changes so that the different color types can be identified. Although nursing seems to cease toward the end of June, the pups remain at the den into September.

While the male travels far to hunt, the vixen remains at home to watch over the pups. Most of the time she is curled up at the den or perhaps a hundred yards away on a prominence. When she wishes to nurse the pups or give them food, she puts her head in the mouth of a burrow and calls softly "mmmmm," "mmmmm." If they do not come forth, she may go to another entrance and call. But usually they respond at once. A sharp, guttural "klung" has the opposite meaning; when the pups hear this warning they scurry into a burrow. This command is of-

Red fox carrying
food to the den
along the park road

ten given after the pups have nursed and the mother wants to go off a short distance to lie down.

The female exhibits extreme friendliness toward her mate. When he returns to the den after an absence she greets him with tail-wagging, face-licking, and much wriggling of her body. He is less demonstrative and acts tired, which he probably is after several hours of hunting. She picks up his offerings—usually mice or ground squirrels—eats her fill or if not hungry, carries the booty to the burrows and calls to the young. He moves off to one side to rest. She sometimes watches for his return from various points. One evening a vixen impatiently moved from one lookout to another for over two hours before the male arrived and received her warm welcome.

Mice and lemmings are the staple all-year food, but in summer the ground squirrel may make up about half the diet. When snowshoe hares and ptarmigan are plentiful, they become prominent in the diet. Carrion is especially attractive in winter, and the fox attends carcasses and curls up on the snow to wait until the wolves and wolverine have eaten. He robs wolf and wolverine catches, and he sometimes has his own caches robbed.

In the latter part of July the foxes go berrying, for they are fond of fruit. Blueberries and crowberries are everywhere available for the picking. The berries are also eaten in winter; sometimes, it is said, quite extensively when mice are scarce.

Foxes appear to be well able to take care of themselves. They can outrun the grizzly, wolf, and wolverine. When the golden eagle swoops at him he stands on watch with his bushy tail erect and straight as a ramrod. The eagle dares not strike.

Lynx

LYNX CANADENSIS

The lynx manner is one of independence, confidence, and complacency. He walks through the woods with dignity, looking neither right nor left. Of course, he is not as oblivious as he appears to be. He may even stop to watch you, but only briefly, and then he continues sedately on his way.

His long legs are thicker than seem necessary to support the lean body, but they are no doubt valuable for long jumps and pouncing. The large, widespreading feet serve him well as snowshoes, and strong, curved claws enable him to scramble readily up a tree. The eyes are startlingly big and yellow and the throat ruff gives to the face a squarish look. Long, glistening black tassels adorn the ears. The stub tail, about four inches long and tipped with black, serves to register emotions. The winter fur is soft and grayish, with few markings except for the facial pattern; the summer coat is more tawny.

Nature has bestowed on the lynx a snowshoe fixation so that he spends his nights and days thinking and dreaming of hare dinners. So dependent has he become on the hare for his main course that his numbers flourish and wane in the wake of hare statistics.

During the period between 1954 and 1956, when lynx were abundant in the park, I made a study of their food habits by analyzing several hundred lynx scats. In addition to hares, the lynx had fed considerably on ptarmigan and in summer on ground squirrels. This part of the diet increased as the hares decreased. But with the decline of the hares, the supplemental foods did not suffice to maintain the population, and the lynx became scarce.

In the winter of 1907-08, Charles Sheldon noted two instances of lynx preying on sheep. The hare population had crashed and the lynx had turned to other sources for survival. One lynx that made its attack on a sheep from ambush found the prey rather large, for in the ensuing

Lynx

struggle he received some severe bruises. He apparently was driven to hunting animals out of his class. About two years after hares disappeared in the Kuskokwim River region a number of years ago, lynx did some preying on reindeer in winter by leaping on their backs and biting the neck. The lynx were said to have attacked the reindeer only that one winter. During periods of food scarcity, lynx have also been observed to prey on each other.

The young are born in May in a cave, or perhaps more often, under a windfall. The gestation period is about sixty days.

In early June, 1955, I saw a lynx in the spruce woods near Savage River. As I stood watching I heard crying sounds up in the woods. The lynx disappeared in the direction of the crying. I followed and saw the parent under a windfall as it was departing with a baby in its mouth, the last of a litter it was moving. Snow and rain had fallen and the mother was carrying her family, one by one, from under an inadequate windfall to another about 250 yards away. The new home was under a brushy spruce that provided a dry shelter in any kind of weather. So well hidden and secure did the mother feel that she barely opened her sleepy eyes even when approached within twenty feet.

How empty the woods and willow patches become with the decline of the hares and the departure of the lynx. It is like an empty stage after the actors have finished their play and departed. Scattered through the quiet woods are their signs of life and activity, but the action has stopped. On the tall willows, six feet from the ground, is the gnawed white hareline, where hares had sat on the snow and gnawed the bark within reach. In places the ground is littered with severed twigs, many of them partially gnawed. And everywhere one encounters tufts of hare fur and hind legs, left on the green moss, signifying hare tragedies and lynx banquets. But the hares will return again to dance in the moonlight, and the lynx will be back in his rich domain walking with stately and regal step.

Wolverine

GULO GULO

The fabulous wolverine is a powerful and picturesque member of the weasel tribe weighing up to thirty-five pounds or more. Because of his stocky build and long hair, he resembles a small bear. Frequently the large hoary marmot is mistaken for him—there is considerable similarity. But the broad yellowish-tan stripe on the sides of the body is distinctive. A whitish collar, not always visible, extends across the throat. The tail is short and bushy; the sharp, well-developed claws are whitish. His range is circumpolar and extends southward in the mountains to Colorado and California, but he is now scarce south of Canada.

The wolverine in late years seems to have become more plentiful in the park; nevertheless, it is always considered something special to see one. They range from river bottom to ridge top and are found in the woods or in open country miles beyond timber. Perhaps because of the open view, he is frequently seen on the low passes, especially on Sable Pass.

In winter the track of the far-wandering wolverine is frequently seen. In his usual gait he bounces along with back arched. Each jump usually leaves a set of three imprints; the one in front is made by a hind foot; the middle imprint is made by a hind foot falling in the track of a front foot; the rear imprint is made by the other front foot. As in the tracks of a hopping rabbit, the hind feet tend to be brought up ahead of the front feet.

The wolverine readily climbs trees. One winter, near a moose carcass, tracks in the snow showed that a wolf had chased a wolverine up a tree on two or three occasions. If the two had met in the open the threatening posture of the wolverine would, no doubt, be sufficient to discourage attack. When attacked by a dog, a wolverine has been seen to lie on its back in a defensive attitude, a position that was effective. Powerful ripping claws and jaws face the attack.

Not much quantitative information has been gathered on his food habits. I have watched him pouncing on mice and suspect that mice (voles) and lemmings are the most important items in his diet. In summer he captures ground squirrels, sometimes by doing some digging. Once I noticed that he had dug out a wasp nest hidden in the ground. The calves of caribou and moose, when very young, are no doubt potential victims. But observations indicate that even a caribou can ward off an attack on the young calves. Such items would, of course, be unimportant in the wolverine's total economy. His wide wanderings in winter would seem to be helpful in finding carrion. In rich wild country, considerable carrion probably comes his way. I have found the wolverine attending a frozen moose carcass for a number of days. When a carcass is not frozen, he carries away what he can to cache for later use.

Wolverine

The gestation period is said to be about nine months. The breeding apparently takes place in summer. The fertilized eggs, after brief development, lie unattached and dormant in the uterus for several months. Some time in midwinter the eggs become attached to the wall of the uterus and the more usual development takes place. (The marten and short-tailed weasel have a similar breeding history.) Females have been found in a nursing condition in early April. Along Igloo Creek, Mr. and Mrs. Edwin C. Park watched a mother nurse two young at least two-thirds grown.

According to Peter Krott, in his fascinating book about the wolverine in Europe, this fierce animal makes a friendly pet. The author, in the beginning, made a business of acquiring young wolverines for sale to zoos. Because the animal was rare and intriguing, the demand was great and the prices remunerative. But Mr. Krott and his wife became fond of the wolverines and found it ever harder to dispose of them. Soon they ceased selling them, and, instead, kept them as pets and allowed them to roam freely over wild country. Studies were made of their habits. Their wolverines might wander far and stay away for several days, but they would return at intervals.

The wolverine is at home in the Denali wilderness. Here we have the rare opportunity of seeing him in his natural environment.

Marten

MARTES AMERICANA

The marten is long and lithe, and its graceful activity is conspicu-
ous. The usual color is a rich brown, shading to blackish on the feet and
tail. The face is grayish with a short, dark line extending upward from
the inner corner of each eye. A large orange throat and breast patch is
very striking in most individuals. The fur is soft and long, the tail is long
and well-furred, and serves to register various emotions. The marten is
alert to sounds and this is indicated by its well-developed, broad ears.

The body is sixteen to seventeen inches long, and the tail, including hair at tips, eight or nine inches. A large male may weigh up to two
and one-half pounds. The female is somewhat smaller than the male.

The marten is found in the forested parts of the park along the
northern and eastern boundary. In winter, I have noted a few tracks in
the big spruce woods south of Wonder Lake. In Wyoming, I have found
martens in rock slides beyond timber, the rock crevasses furnishing the
desired protection.

At one time the marten was thought to depend on the red squirrel
for his daily fare, but recent studies indicate that, ordinarily, relatively
few red squirrels are eaten. A food-habits study made at Castle Rocks
near the northwest corner of the park showed that the martens there
were living primarily on meadow voles and the red-backed vole. Blueberries were eaten in winter as well as in summer. In Wyoming, I have
found martens feeding extensively on blueberry, rhamnus, haw, and
mountain ashberries by choice at a time when voles and other foods
were plentiful. Like the fox and coyote, they have a strong predilection
for berries. In slide rock, they manage to capture an occasional pika.

The marten breeds in July and August, but the young are not born
until nine months later. The long gestation period for such a small animal is due to the delayed attachment of the fertilized egg to the uterus.
Except for the period when the female is followed by young, and during

Marten

the breeding period, martens travel alone.

In Grand Teton Park, Wyoming, where I had much opportunity to observe martens, I found that, although they seldom captured a red squirrel, in their vagabond life over their home area they did use red squirrel homes for sleeping. The marten might spend a few days resting in a squirrel's spare nest, then move on to another squirrel domicile for a few days. The squirrels suffered only the inconvenience of an unwanted guest, and perhaps the temporary loss of a favorite bed.

Mink

MUSTELA VISON

The mink is the amphibious member of the weasel family. He lives along rivers and lakes and probably forages more in the water than on land. Fish, frogs, insects, snails, crayfish, rabbits, muskrats, and mice all appear on his bill of fare. In the country between the mouth of the Yukon and the Kuskokwim River, the mink is said to subsist largely on Alaska blackfish (*Dallia pectoralis*). So abundant were the mink in the area that the Eskimo were called "mink people." The muddy waters in this watery region apparently supported enough blackfish for both the mink and the natives.

Mink tracks have been noted along the Nenana River, but over most of the eastern half of the park the mink is rare.

River Otter

LONTRA CANADENSIS

The otter is rare in the park except in the western portion. Tracks in the snow have been reported at Savage River. It probably occurs in the Nenana River, along the eastern park boundary.

The otter, a member of the weasel family, has become adapted to life in the water. His body is about three feet long, and his long muscular tail is over a foot long. His cousin, the sea otter, plentiful in the Aleutian Islands, is much larger and more specialized for an aquatic life.

I have watched a family of otters in Grand Teton Park fishing for an hour or longer. They kept diving steadily, and occasionally one would come up with a small fish which he would proceed to eat, beginning at the head. Larger fish are taken ashore. Trout, chubs, and suckers were available, but numerous droppings showed that the otter were feeding chiefly on the chubs and suckers. The fish taken were no doubt those most easily captured. A few crayfish were also eaten. This particular family was living in a large beaver house also occupied by beavers. They entered their chamber by land and apparently lived upstairs above the beavers' part of the house with its underwater entrance.

In winter the otter frequently travels over the snow from one piece of water to another. In these travels he slides on his belly down all slopes and sometimes even on the level. In play, a family may repeatedly climb a mudbank or a snowbank to course down a slide leading into water.

Least Weasel

MUSTELA NIVALIS

The range of the least weasel is circumpolar. In North America it is found over most of Alaska and Canada, and southward to Montana, Kansas, and North Carolina. It is widely dispersed, but apparently no-where abundant. This tiny weasel is only six to six and one-half inches long with a maximum tail length of one and one-half inches. It is the smallest living member of the carnivores and weighs no more than a meadow vole. The tail is pure white, lacking the black tip present in other weasels.

I have a record of four specimens from the park. One captured in a mousetrap was five and one-half inches long, the tail measuring less than one inch. I found a dead one at an eagle perch on a ridge top, and remains of two others on gravel bars, apparently discarded after being captured.

A sourdough on the Koyokuk River, with whom my brother and I stayed one night, had a least weasel spending the winter with him. It had the run of the cabin and was very tame.

Apparently the chief food of the least weasel is mice, some of them about as large as himself.

Short-tailed Weasel

(Ermine)

MUSTELA ERMINEA

Two species of weasel occur in the park. The larger one with a black-tipped tail is called the short-tailed weasel, and the smaller one with an extremely short and all-white tail is the least weasel.

Both weasels are brown in summer and white in winter, a protective coloration no doubt useful in escaping detection. In some southern parts of their ranges these weasels remain brown all year, and in intermediate areas part of the population turns white in winter and part of it remains brown. It is apparent that climate has an effect on coat color, the specific factor being the presence or absence of snow on the ground.

It has been pointed out that the short-tailed weasel is much larger in the north than in the southern part of the range. In Wyoming and Colorado, where the tiny least weasel is absent, the short-tailed weasel approaches the least weasel in size and probably fills that weasel's niche in the environment.

The food of the short-tailed weasel probably consists chiefly of various species of meadow mice and lemmings. Observations indicate that ground squirrels and rab-

Short-tailed weasel in winter phase

Short-tailed weasel
in summer phase

bits may occasionally be captured. Shrews no doubt are also on the menu.

In winter, weasel tracks form an odd pattern. Their jumps are alternately long and short, and often they make an erratic trail. Frequently the tracks show that the weasel disappears and travels beneath the surface for a stretch before reappearing.

Even though weasels are not very palatable because of their well-developed musk glands, they nevertheless are often preyed upon. It is a case of coyote or fox capturing any small animal that moves and examining the victim afterwards. Weasels are often left uneaten.

Snowshoe hare in summer phase

Snowshoe Hare

LEPUS AMERICANUS

Like the ptarmigan and the northern weasel, the snowshoe hare (or varying hare) each autumn changes from a dominantly brown summer coat to a white winter ensemble. (In Washington where snow is scarce in its habitat, the snowshoe hare remains brown the year round.) His coat color blends at all seasons with his background, so all he need do to be fairly sure of escaping visual detection is to have confidence in his camouflage and sit motionless. The fur is so long, thick, and warm that he can sit all day in fifty below zero weather without freezing. His large hind legs are equipped with snowshoe feet, an obvious advantage in snow country.

Snowshoe hare
in winter phase

The most favorable hare habitat is the brushy country along the east and north boundaries. Here a few may always be found. Out in the park they are quite scarce except in those years when the population is at or near a peak.

In winter, the hares feed on bark gnawed from various shrubs and saplings. Willow, dwarf birch, and alder, because of their high palatability and abundance, are especially important winter foods. In years of hare abundance, I have seen patches of willow and dwarf birch trimmed to the snow line. At such times large willow brush may show a white band two feet wide where the hares have gnawed the bark within reach of the snow line. As the snow deepens, some foods are buried, but the change of level brings new food supplies within reach. A variety of other shrubs are also eaten at this season. Spruce bark is relished. Porcupines and also red squirrels feeding in a spruce tree inadvertently add to the hare menu many dropped spruce twigs. In summer, the hares turn to a variety of fresh green foods.

The young of the snowshoe hare are furred and active when born and apparently there is no real nest provided. (In the cottontail branch of the family the young are born hairless, helpless, and in a warm nest.)

The litters are weaned (in captivity) when about four weeks old. The females breed again soon after a litter is born. It seems likely that a female may have as many as three or four litters during a summer. A male is apparently with a female for only a short time.

A number of animals are subject to cycles of extreme abundance and scarcity. The pendulum swings from one extreme to the other. A population, in spite of enemies of all kinds, increases until the numbers become so large that they threaten the food supply or, because of congestion, are drastically reduced by diseases. The length of cycle in a species depends upon annual losses and the rate of increase. Cycles are relatively short in voles and lemmings which breed at an early age (a few weeks), breed often, and have large litters. In these small rodents the cycle may cover a span of about four years. In larger species, the cycles are longer.

The snowshoe hare is one of the more obvious examples of a cyclic species. From acute scarcity the population in about ten years pyramids until the country is full of hares. The woods are alive with a variety of activity. Enterprise, lovemaking, and tragedy are at their peak. Not only have the hares multiplied, but their enemies have flourished, and the lynx, fox, wolverine, and birds of prey have all prospered, and certain enemies such as the lynx become especially abundant.

During the high hare population peak, between 1953 and 1955, a few dead hares began to appear in the summer of 1954. In early August a group of tourists on a short walk noted three dead hares in the hotel area. But the hares were still numerous in the spring of 1955 and I anticipated the woods alive with young hares the following months. Instead, they decreased. By July, along Igloo Creek, they had become scarce. The so-called hare crash had taken place.

Nature steps into all situations, and one control or another automatically appears. Food shortage, disease, predation, or competition enter the picture. Adjusting is a continuous process. Many people are talking and writing about the human population explosion in our midst, fearing that space for ourselves and nature is disappearing alarmingly. Perhaps we should consider the snowshoe hare.

Pika

OCHOTONA COLLARIS

The pika, cony, or rock rabbit, as he is variously called, makes his home in rock slides. His way of life, and his physical attributes, are such, that he would have difficulty surviving away from the labyrinth of passages in his slide rock home.

The pika is in the same order (different family) as hares and rabbits. Like rabbits, they have two pairs of upper incisors; back of the grooved anterior incisors is a pair of very small incisors. The feet are furred; the ears are not long but are rounded and prominent. Something has happened to the external tail for there is none. The tail vertebrae lie under the body skin. The plump body is about six or seven inches long as the cony sits on a rock; the color is gray.

Pika

The call is a single nasal "yank," usually uttered while perched on a rock where he can look around. He may be difficult to locate, but a movement as he disappears in a crevice and reappears on the same rock or one nearby will reveal him. Usually other calls from various parts of the rock field will indicate the location of other pikas.

The pika is known for his hay making in preparation for the long winter. During much of the summer he is busy carrying grass, herbs, and twigs to his many caches located in cavities protected from the weather. The vegetation is usually added slowly enough to the various caches so that it all cures properly. Only occasionally is a cache moldy. I have noted a few caches composed of the broad, heavy coltsfoot leaves that had failed to dry properly; possibly these slow-drying leaves were harvested in wet weather. Nearly all plants within range of his rocky habitat are used. Willow, rose, grass, sedge, horsetail, various saxifrages, fireweed, coltsfoot, fruiticose, and even crustose lichens are some of the many plants that have been found in the caches. Some books say that the hay is spread over rocks to dry and then stored. The pika's technique is superior to such quick drying, and results in more nutritious and greener hay.

The sheep, moose, and caribou often seek mineral licks consisting of clay which can be readily eaten. Ground squirrels and marmot feed on pebbles or fine dust in their craving for minerals. On one occasion I watched a pika gnawing a rock. A niche showed that a considerable amount of it had been eaten. I carried the rock away as a sample of rock-eating but later thought better of it and returned it to the pika. Perhaps in the future I may be able to check the rock again.

Along the road, the first good place to look for pikas is in the jumble of rocks above the Savage River Bridge, an accumulation that has fallen away from a rocky point, part of which is still in place. On Polychrome Pass are several rock fields where many pikas are living. Another pika place along the road is a mile or two beyond Eielson Visitor Center. A pretty picture is a pika carrying a bouquet of flowers, neatly arranged, as though he were going a-courting.

Hoary Marmot

MARMOTA CALIGATA

The hoary marmot is an amplified version of the eastern wood-chuck. It is roughly bicolor, being gray over the shoulder region and light brown over the hips. The black patch across the nose enhances its facial aspect somewhat, and the jet-black feet add a little contrast to its appearance. He has a bushy tail that jerks about a good deal, especially when he travels. Occasionally, he is mistaken for a wolverine. His soft color pattern is an excellent example of camouflage and of this he apparently is aware as he flattens himself on a rock to escape detection.

His voice is exceptional. One day, some years ago, I walked down Savage Canyon with two companions. One of them, who stopped to photograph some flowers, was left far behind. When he finally overtook us he said that he had heard us whistling and had hurried as best he could. We said we had not whistled, but he was still sure he had heard us. Then it dawned on me that he had been hearing the loud, piercing, prolonged warning whistles of the marmots that make their homes in the canyon. This whistle is one of the familiar sounds in marmot country. The approach of a fox, grizzly bear, or golden eagle is announced by loud whistling which alerts everyone, including ground squirrels and mountain sheep, to be on their guard.

One day three of us watched a youngish marmot high on a sheep ridge. He was apprehensive and for a time whistled at intervals. When one of my companions whistled in the same key, the marmot answered. But if the imitation were off key there was no reply. The marmot responded for as long as our patience held. This instance may have been exceptional, for I have had no opportunity as yet to make additional observations.

The marmot has learned to seek a home in a rock fortress as a safeguard against being excavated by a grizzly. Whenever possible the dens are dug in rocky areas, or at rock outcrops. One den on a steep slope that I observed for several years was enlarged and renovated each year. The small rocks encountered in the digging were carried out in the mouth and dropped on the edge of the mound. In late summer, mouthfuls of dry grass are carried in for the winter hibernating nest. One look at the broad, fat marmot suggests that he could sleep for a long time without food. When he retires, he may plug the entrance with rocks and mud.

The home life of the marmots has not been carefully studied, but they seem to live in colonies, all using a number of dens distributed as much as 200 yards or more apart. I have seen several adults in a colony and watched them move from one den to another. In traveling between some of the dens the marmots are highly vulnerable if surprised by one of their enemies. The attractive black-eyed young required two or more years to gain the dimensions and weight of their elders.

Two excellent places to find marmots along the highway are the jumbled boulders on the east end of the Savage River bridge and in Polychrome Pass, especially on a gray, lichen-covered rock below the road and the rocky ridge across the ravine from it. If not active, the marmots may generally be seen flattened out on a rock, basking in the sunshine.

Marmot

Some of the marmots in these places and also in remote areas are quite tame. I walked practically alongside one big marmot as it fed in a patch of mertensia. It gobbled up dozens of the big leaves and chewed them down lustily and noisily, scarcely regarding my presence. Accustomed to harmless mountain sheep and caribou, they sometimes apparently place humans in the same category.

Arctic Ground Squirrel

SPERMOPHILUS PARRYII

The most neighborly animals in the park are the ground squirrels. They quickly become tame at cabins and campgrounds and early stuff their cheek pouches with hotcakes until their gulps become ludicrous with excessive efforts to make room for one more mouthful. Leave a cabin door ajar and the bread supply is soon being appropriated.

Ground squirrels are always standing erect shouting worried warnings of danger. Much of the time the cries seem to be only an outlet for accumulated nervousness. But one learns to differentiate these cries from those delivered in dead earnest. When extreme anxiety is unmistakable, it pays to become alert. Their cries have often served to call my attention to passing grizzlies, wolves, foxes, lynx, and low-flying eagles. And the whole wildlife community similarly benefits. The message is relayed in all directions by ground squirrels in a sort of chain reaction, but emphasis in delivery gradually decreases until the message is lost. The cheery calls and sharp warnings of the ground squirrels are, for many of us, closely associated with the general flavor and enhancement of the north country.

The winter months are spent hibernating in a burrow, curled up in a grass nest. A few squirrels remain active until the middle of October or even later. In the spring some come forth in April. Where deep snowfields cover the dens and it seems unlikely that much temperature change could penetrate to the squirrels, they nevertheless awaken as though provided with alarm clocks and tunnel to the surface. Their muddy tracks radiate from each den over the snow as the squirrels seek exposed forage.

General observations indicate that the female has only one litter each breeding season. The young do not reach adult size by the first autumn. Year after year, the ground squirrel population in the park is high. Yet no indication of cyclic behavior has been observed. Possibly their many enemies prevent them from becoming superabundant and, therefore, subject to epidemic disease.

Ground squirrels are an important factor in the park ecology. They furnish about 90 percent of the golden eagle's diet, and in some localities they are the chief food of the gyrfalcon. The wolf at times feeds exclusively on them, and they contribute heavily, sometimes 50 percent, to the fox diet. The information available indicates that the wolverine often captures them, and with the disappearance of the hares, the lynx deigns to hunt them for a season. For the grizzly they furnish his most dependable taste of meat. The bears spend many hours excavating for ground squirrels.

Arctic ground squirrel

Red Squirrel

TAMIASCIURUS HUDSONICUS

The noisy red squirrel, with his churring, chattering, and "sic-sic-ing," lends a touch of the familiar to the northern woods. He has followed the spruces along the rivers to timberline, and I saw one a half-mile beyond timber, living, perhaps temporarily, among the pikas in tumbled rocks. They are generally plentiful, but in 1956 I found them extremely scarce. A catastrophic die-off had apparently occurred in the park, and that year the squirrels were also reported scarce in other parts of Alaska.

These northern squirrels have a spruce cone economy. Even before the middle of August they are frantically harvesting spruce cones (chiefly white spruce in the park). One afternoon a squirrel worked steadily in a group of spruces for almost three hours, cutting cones and giving them a flip with his mouth or paws. Hundreds were scattered about under the trees, and still they continued to rain and strike the ground with dull thuds. Occasionally the squirrel seemed to get his wires crossed and, instead of dropping a cone, would run all the way down the trunk with it.

Sometimes twigs bearing a cluster of cones are nipped off. In two or three sizeable caches all the cones were in clusters still attached to twigs. Perhaps this rather efficient method of handling cones is at times accentuated by certain individuals.

In September I have seen many caches scattered about on the forest floor as though piled hurriedly as a temporary expedient. One heap measured five feet long, three feet wide, and about seven inches deep. Possibly these heaps were later stored more carefully in secluded spots with the tips of the cones pointed downward. After the cones are stored, the squirrels continue to give them solicitous care. One spring when melting snow exposed a cache of cones, they were re-cached in various places, but each cone was first bitten into, and if spoiled was discarded. About the same time another cache of cones in a burrow was also removed and stored elsewhere.

Red squirrel in spruce

Another food item that is stored in quantity is the mushroom. Many are placed on spruce branches where, if they do get wet, they will soon dry out and remain edible, and I once found great quantities stored in a cabin.

Aside from the cached foods, the red squirrels feed extensively, at least through the winter and spring, on the buds of spruce twigs. Often you may find many twigs on the ground with the tiny buds neatly removed. In Wyoming, I have found squirrels in summer living for days on the larvae in balsom poplar galls, and I suspect such food may be eaten in Alaska, too, where galls are found.

Each squirrel commonly has two or more nests built of grasses, shredded bark, ptarmigan feathers, and hair of hares, moose, or whatever is available.

The squirrel piles this material on a branch until it is two or three feet high. One squirrel that I watched building a nest pushed himself into the middle of the heap. Soon the whole nest shook vigorously at intervals. Apparently he was forming a chamber.

The chatter of red squirrels, their piles of middens, and their busy harvesting activities add cheer and life to the northern woods.

Northern Flying Squirrel

GLAUCOMYS SABRINUS

When the gesticulating red squirrel has finished his daylight bustling and retires to his nest, the flying squirrel comes forth to take over the night, but in a gentle and quiet manner. Like the night-flying owl, its coat is soft and its flight silent.

The furred "wing" membranes on each side of the body are attached to the full length of the fore and hind legs and are supported and extended in part by a cartilaginous process growing out from the wrist. Thus when the legs are extended laterally, the squirrel becomes a glider with the most delicate and reliable controls. His sailing carries him from the top of one tree to the base of another where he checks his speed by an upward swing and alights with a soft thud. Sharp claws and squirrel agility give him the climbing ability to get quickly up a tree. When trees are widely spaced as they are in some stands of large balsam poplar, he may in winter make a five-point landing in the snow, his broad thickly-furred tail serving as rudder and gliding surface, and to a less extent as a landing ski. I have seen tracks showing a touch and a raise before the final landing with legs drawn under; then follow long jumps over the snow to the nearest tree. The nest is usually built in a tree cavity. Perhaps the height of night esthetics is lying in a sleeping bag under the open sky, the stars and moon lighting up the spaces between the trees, and watching a family of flying squirrels gliding overhead in their nightplay, their shadowy forms silhouetted against the moonlit sky.

Northern flying squirrel

Porcupine

ERETHIZON DORSATUM

The porcupine has been accused of being slow-witted, but we must admit that he has not done badly for he is able to lead an unhurried life in the country. His quill protection has, no doubt, decreased his need for mental activity, and his eyesight does seem deficient. But his hearing is quite keen, and judging by his nose activity it appears that his sense of smell is on the acute side. His mental and physical attributes are all based on the quill.

The upper surface of the porcupine, except for the vulnerable face, is covered with several hundred ivory-colored quills, touched with black or brown, and reaching a length up to at least two and one-half inches. They are needle-sharp and just back from the tip are numerous minute barbs. When the quill enters the flesh of an enemy, any muscular movement causes the quill to move forward until it emerges on the opposite side or becomes lodged against the bone or under the hide.

When the porcupine senses danger he raises the quills on his back and has his muscular spine-studded tail in readiness to flip upward. He tries to keep his rear toward the enemy and to push his head into protective brush. The quills are loosely attached to the skin so pull out readily when they stick into anything. The underside of the body, in addition to the face, lacks quills but because of the short legs, the belly region is close to the ground and not vulnerable unless the porcupine is flipped over on his back. I knew a sled dog that sometimes killed porcupines by weaving and maneuvering until he had the opportunity to grasp the vulnerable nose and thus avoid the quills. Wolves, coyotes, and wolverines feed on porcupines; possibly they use a similar technique in overcoming the quill armor.

In winter the porcupine feeds extensively on the inner bark and the needles of conifers. The patches where the bark has been removed are a common sight in porcupine woods. The spruces, in the last stand of timber on the east side of the Toklat River along the road, were nearly all killed by girdling, many of them back in the 1920s when the porcupine population was extremely high. This scraggly woods is a favorite nesting area for merlins, kestrels, black-billed magpies, and northern shrikes so that porcupine activity that seemed generally harmful has been highly beneficial to these species. Many porcupines spend the winter in a willow patch beyond the spruce and subsist on willow. For shelter in winter a windfall, hollow tree, or an old fox or wolf den may be used. Several may take residence under a cabin.

In spring I have watched porcupines climbing clumsily in tall willow brush feeding on the swollen buds. Swaying on a limb, he reaches for a slender branch, pulls it to him, and passes the length of it past his nose to discover the buds which he nips off. If the branch is obstreperous and cannot readily be handled in this manner, he severs it with his rodent incisors and then removes the buds as his paws manipulate the

Porcupine in tree

twig past his jaws. The new shoots of fireweed and other herbs are avidly sought in early summer. Willow leaves are included in the varied summer diet.

The breeding season is in the fall and the young are born about seven months later. The usual single young one weighs about a pound, almost as much as a newborn grizzly. The eyes are open, the short spines are evident, and protective reactions are soon functioning.

Their voice development is quite obvious when one or more porcupines resides under a cabin. The night moanings, squeaks of irritability, cluckings, and caressing sounds are enough to keep even the exhausted hiker awake.

Muskrat

ONDATRA ZIBETHICUS

In some parts of Alaska where extensive favorable pond habitat prevails, muskrats are abundant and their sedge lodges are part of the scenery. In the park there are a few muskrats in Horseshoe Lake and other ponds and creeks near the eastern border, and also in the Wonder Lake area. These usually live in bank burrows with submerged entrances. It is not uncommon to find a muskrat living in an occupied beaver house, apparently utilizing an unoccupied cranny. They ply back and forth across the pond, just as the beavers do, and submerge with a mouthful of sedge which they are taking to the young. At Wonder Lake, I have seen muskrats swimming under the little bridge across the stream inlet, carrying sedges to young that were kept in a burrow in a nearby bank of the lake.

Because muskrats are associated with beavers they are sometimes mistaken for young beavers. The longer scaly tail, that is flattened vertically rather than horizontally, serves as a certain identification. The muskrat is also much quicker in its actions, and is smaller than any beaver old enough to be abroad.

The muskrat's chief food consists of green vegetation (various water plants and sedges) and clams when available; it has even been reported catching small fish in some regions. Some of the deeper water plants it secures by diving, and in the spring I have watched them climb onto the ice to eat them. A muskrat looks very tiny sitting on the ice beside a big beaver.

Muskrat have their winged and four-footed enemies. Mink, living in the same environment, prey on them, but not indiscriminately. Other carnivores such as the fox, coyote, and wolf might encounter one on land, but chiefly by accident.

Muskrat

Beaver

CASTOR CANADENSIS

Beavers may be found at Horseshoe Lake, Riley Creek, various ponds near the Nenana River, and in ponds and creeks along the road in the Wonder Lake region. They are out chiefly at night, but many families emerge for pond activity by 2 or 3 o'clock in the afternoon.

Beavers are large rodents, scaling sixty pounds or more. Their weight does not make them good hikers, but it is no handicap in water where they paddle their way about as though they were skiffs. And when they sit up to gnaw down an aspen or cottonwood, a favorite pastime, a good solid fulcrum might be a comfortable advantage. The broad, flat, scaly tail serves as a prop when sitting erect, as a rudder when swimming, and for sounding an alarm (by slapping water) when an enemy is discovered.

The front feet are equipped with five strong toes which serve well as hands for holding twigs as the animal feeds on bark. The claws function well in all digging operations, and the arms suffice for holding gobs of mud against the chest as he pushes the load onto the dam or house. Occasionally, he carries mud in his arms as he walks up the house roof on hind legs.

The hind feet are large and webbed for swimming. Even the nails on the toes are flattened in keeping with the swimming needs. The nail of the second hind claw is double and the nail of the first toe fits down on a hard pad and is movable like a duck's bill. These specialized claws are used for combing the fur and possibly for removing some of the large beetles that live in the fur. The prominent incisors, used for gnawing, grow continuously, as they do in all rodents, in order to compensate for wear. This is an especially fortunate adaptation for the beaver, who does so much gnawing. Otherwise his teeth would soon be worn to the gums. If an incisor for any reason is thrown out of line, so it has no surface to bite against and wear, it will become excessively elongated as it grows in a curve.

A flourishing beaver colony apparently consists of the parents, the young of the year, and the previous year's offspring. It is for this reason that we often discover three sizes of beaver in a pond. Much of beaver activity involves cooperative projects where there is latitude for any amount of individual initiative. The dam or dams must be built, or raised, or kept in repair. The house, located either in the pond, or partially or wholly on the shore, may require additional sticks, and toward autumn is plastered on the outside with wet mud as a sort of annual renovation. This "stucco" winterizes the lodge. Occasionally, it is decided that a new house is needed and that gives young and old plenty to do. Some beavers along Riley Creek live in bank burrows and build no dams or houses.

The most effective dam that has come to my attention was built at the outlet of Wonder Lake in 1960; it raised the water level of the lake over two feet. For many days the outlet stream was dry. The water held back in the lake amounted to well over one hundred million cubic feet or over seven billion pounds of water.

Beaver feeding

The water depth beside the lodge must be deepened if too shallow, so that the underwater entrance to the lodge is deep enough to keep from freezing over and imprisoning the occupants. Also a certain depth of water is needed beside the lodge in which to store the brush pile that is the winter food supply. Another activity practiced extensively by some colonies is the building of canals, some of which may have great length. The mud from the digging is deposited along the canal forming a raised border. These waterways are useful for general travel to food areas and for transporting branches and poles.

The favorite foods of the beaver include willow, aspen, cottonwood, and alder. Willow brush re-sprouts readily and grows rapidly, and therefore maintains itself better than some of the other foods. Also it flourishes in the wet habitat created by the beaver ponds.

Where beavers create ponds with their dams, they produce a habitat for fish, ducks, muskrats, shore birds, moose, and many other forms of water and shore life. In Wyoming, I have observed the dead trees, killed by flooding, used by herons for nesting, and one of the heron nests was later used by a pair of geese.

The rich, warm coat of the beaver has long been worn by both humans and beavers, but the beaver wears it best.

Shrews

Shrews may be identified by their long, pointed, mobile nose, extremely minute eyes, short velvety fur, and blackish-tipped teeth. They are the smallest mammals in the world, some kinds weighing less than three grams. It would require over one hundred of these to weigh one pound. Because of the shrew's small size and long nose, Alaskans frequently refer to them as long-nosed mice.

Thousands of shrews (five species) are vigorously active in the park, but are rarely seen. Occasionally, one may be discovered crossing an open area, like a mechanical toy, or one may flash from cover and as quickly disappear. They share with the voles and lemmings the shade and darkness of the hidden runways beneath the moss and grassy cover. Here they are active predators, darting about in their search for prey. With nervous activity they examine their microhabitat in search of insects and other invertebrates. Spiders flee in haste when the presence of a shrew is sensed. Their hunting technique appears to consist of random movements until they collide with their victim. They no doubt depend chiefly upon the sense of smell in recognizing their prey.

Shrews eat often and a great deal. In captivity, a shrew weighing 3.6 grams ate over three times its weight of food daily. Any kind of meat attracts shrews, as many Alaskans have learned when discovering their meat caches invaded by them. The energetic activity of shrews suggests the need for rapid metabolism and plentiful supply of body fuel.

Although shrews are active throughout the winter, they nevertheless appear to be delicately attuned to their environment. They seem to be especially susceptible to chilling, perhaps because of their tiny body and short fur. Winter temperatures in the north are severe, but ground temperatures under the snow blanket are rather moderate. Shrews perhaps require only a warm nest—their intense activity keeping them warm when foraging.

Shrews are not rated high gastronomically by many mammals. This is apparently due to the hip glands which have a strong, pungent odor. But their lack of palatability does not give them much protection. If, for instance, a fox locates a faint sound in the grass, he pounces and learns later what he has caught. If the prey is a shrew, it may be left where killed by the fox, carried a short way and dropped, or during denning time even brought home to the den before being discarded. I have often found shrew carcasses lying uneaten about fox dens. Birds of prey feed more extensively on them, possibly because of their poorly developed sense of smell and sense of taste. Grayling, and also trout, have been found with one or more shrews in their stomachs. At Moose Creek, several grayling were taken which had eaten shrews, one having eaten three of them. This indicates that the species captured readily enter the water. One species, the water shrew (*Sorex palustris*), recently found in the park, is specialized for aquatic life.

The shrew population is apparently cyclic for there are years when they are very abundant, followed by years of extreme scarcity.

Five kinds of shrews are in the park. They differ from one another in several respects, but may be fairly well identified by tail length alone. The masked shrew (*Sorex cinereus*) has a tail averaging about thirty-nine millimeters long; the tail of the dusky shrew (*Sorex monticolus*) averages

about forty-eight mm.; and that of the rare pygmy shrew (*Sorex hoyi*), thirty-one mm. The average length of tail of the Arctic shrew (*Sorex arcticus*) is about thirty-six mm., overlapping slightly in this measurement with that of the masked shrew, but the rich chocolate color of the Arctic shrew will identify it.

Arctic shrew

The Mouse World

MICROTINAE

Are there any trails in the park? Yes, thousands of miles, but most of them are under a canopy of grass and sphagnum moss and are only one or two inches wide, so of course they are not of much use to you.

And even if we could nibble on Alice's mushroom and grow, in reverse, small enough to use them, we would hardly dare, at least a lady wouldn't, for she would soon meet a mouse, inasmuch as these trails have been constructed by, and belong to, mice. And I might add that the fierce little shrews use them too. Where the trails cross green, mossy carpets and enter tiny exquisite nooks I imagine one might also meet a few northern fairies.

Brown lemming

Seven kinds of mice (voles and lemmings) are known to live in the park. Some of these are quite outstanding for one thing or another, and possibly all of them are, if we only knew more about them. However, we do know that they are all important.

———

I am best acquainted with the hay mouse, or singing vole (*Microtus miurus*) because some of my field observations led me to him. Some years ago I kept finding many caches of dried vegetation, some caches large enough to fill a bushel basket. This hay was always kept either off the ground or under cover. It was placed at the base of willows in the basket formed by the many stems, or on a surface spruce root, in a rock niche, or under a log. Pikas are known to make hay, but no such activity has been reported for mice. Pikas were not involved, for they live in the talus rock, and these caches were mostly far from pika habitat. After considerable effort, I learned that a yellowish-brown field mouse was the interesting haymaker. The hay is put up for winter use. The sign showed that sometimes a snowshoe hare has found a cache and helped himself.

In addition to hay, this mouse also stores roots in underground cellars that he excavates, and the roots are not thrown in helter-skelter, at least not in most of the caches I examined. The black, round nutlike tubers of the horsetail were in one pile, coltsfoot underground stems in another, and carrotlike roots of a pedicularis in still another. An interesting feature was the structure of some of the tunnels which were built in the form of a pearl necklace. Tiny passages, just large enough for the body of the mouse to squeeze through, joined the cavities or, so to speak, the "pearls." In addition to all of these accomplishments, these mice do much miniature warbling, enough so they have been called singing voles.

The tail is short, measuring slightly over one inch; the body length averages about five inches. It is found from moist lowland habitats to ridge tops.

––––––––

The large, plump, and richly colored brown lemming (*Lemmus sibiricus*) is notorious for his overpopulation problem. On some occasions they migrate in hordes, even into the ocean in some parts of their circumpolar home. The lemming is cyclic in the park, but usually only to about the same degree as the other mice. However, in the low part of the cycle, they may become extremely scarce, more so than do the voles. The brown lemming does not turn white in winter as does its relative, the collared lemming (over most of its range). The body is about five and one-half inches long and the tail is just under one inch. The thumb claw consists of a three-pronged flat nail. A large lemming weighs about one-quarter pound. They are widely distributed in both open tundra and woods where the habitat is not too dry.

––––––––

The northern bog lemming (*Synaptomys borealis*) is usually not thought of as a true lemming, but it does belong to the lemming tribe. It has a short tail, less than one inch long; the body length is about four inches; the upper incisors have a vertical groove near the outer edge;

and the males have a white spot on each side marking the location of hip glands. The thumb claw is a broad nail, in this respect resembling the brown lemming. The distribution of this mouse is spotty. It was taken in the Wonder Lake area in a wet grass and sedge habitat just inside a spruce woods.

———

The yellow-cheeked vole (*Microtus xanthognathus*), the largest mouse in the park, has a body length of six or seven inches, tail length of about two inches, and weighs up to about six ounces. These mice live in isolated colonies, but where found may be abundant. Not recorded in the park since 1907 when it was abundant along the Toklat River.

———

The tundra vole (*Microtus oeconomus*) is a large vole, widely distributed, and is especially fond of dense grass or sedge habitats. Its body length is five to five and one-half inches, and tail length a little less than two inches. Its brownish-gray color is similar to the common meadow mouse.

———

The meadow vole (*Microtus pennsylvanicus*) is common in interior Alaska, so far as known, but is rare in the park. With more investigation, it may be found plentiful in places along the north boundary. This is a common vole over much of Canada and the Rocky Mountain, central, and eastern states. It prefers moist habitats. The body length is about five inches, tail about two inches, and the color is dark brown.

Red-backed vole

———

The northern red-backed vole (*Clethrionomys rutilus*) lives in both the open tundra and the woods. Generally, it has a reddish back, but in a dark color phase, the back is blackish. These mice are fond of berries, their teeth being stained blue during the blueberry season. They also feed on seeds, stems, and leaves.

———

The several species of mice vary in abundance from year to year. In places where some of them have been studied, a well-defined three- or four-year cycle has been noted. The mouse populations have a tremendous influence on our wildlife economy. Foxes, martens, weasels, owls, hawks, and a host of others feed extensively on this fauna and react to its abundance. When the lemming increase in the north, the snowy owls (and others) increase, and when the lemming become scarce, these owls come south in search of food and we have the snowy owl invasions, especially in north-central and eastern states. In 1955, when mice were abundant, the hawk owls in the park reached a high point, but again became scarce when the mouse population dropped.

Bat

VESPERTILIONIDAE

A bat was reported in flight at Wonder Lake in 1959 and again in 1960. Since no specimen has been examined there is no definite identification, but judging from the geographical distribution of bats it seems probable that those seen in the park belong to the genus Myotis. Three or four species of this genus are known to occur in southeastern Alaska. The little brown bat (*Myotis lucifugus*) has been taken at Illiamna Lake at the base of the Alaska Peninsula, so it seems likely that this is the bat seen at Wonder Lake.

Grizzly print